100 TIMELESS MONEY SAVING TIPS

for the average man and woman

LATANYA OATES HICKS

CreateSpace

A DBA of On-Demand Publishing, LLC

4900 LaCross Road

North Charleston, SC 29406

Design and typography by CreateSpace

Library of Congress Cataloging-in-Publication Data

  Hicks, LaTanya Oates

100 Timeless Money Saving Tips

ISBN: 1-4802-3926-7

ISBN-13: 978-1-4802-3926-5

This publication is designed to provide information with regard to the subject matter covered. It is sold with the understanding that the publisher is not engaged in rendering legal, accounting, or other professional advice. If legal advice or other expert assistance is required, the services of a competent professional person should be sought.

Printed in the United States of America

ACKNOWLEDGEMENTS

I would like to thank my hero, Jason Aaron Hicks, my favorite son. Jason is my biggest supporter and encourager in all of my projects. I see the reflection of myself in him many times. Now he reminds me of the lessons in life.

My sister group SWAP (Sisters With A Purpose – Akiba Aliyy, Jackie Jefferson, Janet Nah, Linette Dudley, Susan King and Wendy Barber) have also supported and encouraged my forward movement in having this book published.

The book would not be complete if I did not give thanks for my mother, father and brother, Bill Oates. Although, mom and dad have made their transitions, they are still very present in my life in all I do.

I would be remiss if I did not thank the many friends, family members, and clients who have allowed me the privilege of helping them meet their short and long-term financial goals. Your trust in me is invaluable and is one of the primary catalysts for this book.

Last, but surely not least, I am thankful for the support of the Universe, who we also call God in my life. This project has been an amazing journey of discovery and more joy in my life than I could have ever humanly planned.

CONTENTS

CONTENTS

INTRODUCTION

"100 Timeless Money Saving Tips"
for the average man and woman

Ever thought about saving money? What about bringing your spending in line with your income? Do you want to be debt free and live comfortably too? How often have you tried to attain these goals, but gave up because they seem impossible? It is possible to live well, while staying within your means, and I have some practical, painless suggestions that will help you get there!

Hi, my name is LaTanya Oates Hicks and I am a Budget Solutions Consultant and Certified Credit Counselor, living in the sunny state of Florida! For years, I showed family members and friends how to better manage their money and live the good life...debt free! As a professional counselor and author, I am able to teach my proven, money saving tips to countless others and help free them from the burden of personal debt.

So, you may be wondering where I acquired this financial practicality. I come from a middleclass family with a mother who could not hold on to a dollar without it burning her hands and a father who would hold onto the dollar until the eagle squealed or the president choked to death! Needless to say, my saving habits are derived from my dad, while my appreciation for the finer things in life come directly from mom. My friends jokingly refer to me as fiscally conservative, which is the politically correct term for calling me a cheapskate! My family members also admire my money saving ability, unfortunately, they also like to think of me as the local ATM because they know that over the years I have acquired a healthy savings account.

On the surface, I am your average single woman in her early 50s, with an average annual income around $40,000. However, unlike others living paycheck-to-paycheck, I own my own home, car and a few of what I call luxury items. I travel to exotic places, I love going to the movies, I eat out about once a week and manage the other bills that most people have: cable, cell phone, utilities and credit cards. You can see that I do not earn a great deal of money by typical standards, but I often have money left over to splurge a little at the end of each month and save some for a rainy day. Most importantly, I have the "Peace of Mind" that comes from managing my finances in a practical and sustainable way.

While I cannot change your attitudes and feelings, I can provide you with some easy to implement, money saving strategies that will help you acquire financial peace of mind. I always say, "If I can do it, anybody can!" Let's start with the end in mind and work to the #1 money saving tip. Get ready, get set, start saving now!

GENERAL TIPS
100-98

Tip #100

When you see money, usually pennies in the street, on the sidewalk, in the grass, around your house, pick them up. They add up to be dollars. Also, once you arrive home in the evening or at least once a week, empty your purse/pockets of all your change into a small decorative container along with the money you find on the sidewalks. Remember to offer a thought of appreciation for the money placed in the container. You'd be surprised what the thought does and how the coins add up at the end of the month. This money can go towards a bill, for Christmas gifts, birthday gifts, gas for the car, or to treat the family for dinner out at the end of the month.

Tip #99

Sometimes it's frightening to think of not having a house phone, but nowadays most people don't. If you have an alarm system connected to a land line, don't worry. Wi-Fi service is available (there may be an additional expense, but in the long run, the money you save disconnecting the land line will pay for the Wi-Fi connection). If you are using a fax line with a home phone line, now you can use the internet/email for the service. We are a mobile society. If you don't really use your home phone, cancel it and just keep the cell phone. It will be a lot less expensive. Consider the 'Pay As You Go' phones as they have no contracts.

Tip #98

Along with the home phone, most people get a package deal with their phone, to include cable or internet. Don't be fooled. Break up the package, downgrade on the cable (unless you are a television enthusiast) to the basics, and keep the high speed internet, your gateway to keeping in touch with others in your world. Your phone company or cable company make more money off of the bundles because usually you, the customer, do not utilize all three.

GREEN HOUSE TIPS

"Green" House Saving Tips: Sometimes buying the eco-friendly products can get expensive.

Tips 97-86 are techniques which are green-friendly on the environment and your wallet.

Tip #97

(Green) Furniture and floor polish:

1. Dip a cloth in cool black tea and clean wood furniture surfaces with a solution of 1 part lemon juice to 2 parts vegetable oil.

2. Cleaning wood floors: use a damp sponge or microfiber mop to wash wood floors with warm water. If extra dirty, mix 1/8 cup liquid dishwashing soap with 1/8 cup white vinegar in a 4L (1 gallon) bucket of warm water.

3. Mopping vinyl flooring: use a mixture that is 50/50 water and vinegar (white). Do not use on wood or imitation wood floors.

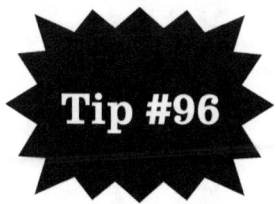

Tip #96

(Green) Silver Cleaner:

Use toothpaste to shine the silverware and ketchup to polish the copper.

Tip #95

(Green) Glass and Window Cleaner:

Mix 1 part hot water with 1 part vinegar in a reusable spray bottle. If tough dirt – add a drop of dishwashing liquid to the mix. Wipe clean with a microfiber cloth to avoid paper waste.

Tip #94

(Green) All-Purpose Cleaner:

Mix 2 tablespoons dishwashing liquid to 2 cups of water in a spray bottle. For tougher jobs – mix a paste of baking soda and water to gently scrub grimy counter tops, stained sinks, or appliances that are scratch proof. Use an old toothbrush to clean corners and cracks and a generic Magic Eraser or micro-fiber cloth to wipe clean.

Tip #93

(Green) Oven Cleaner:

Mix 1 part baking soda to 3 parts hot water to make a thick paste. Coat the oven surface with the paste, let sit overnight. Use a plastic spatula (metal will scratch) to remove your greasy oven grime. Line your oven bottom with a spilmat oven liner or aluminum foil to prevent future buildup. Be sure to wipe the oven clean after each splatter, spill, or bubble-over.

Tip #92

(Green) Microwave Oven Cleaner:

Heat ½ cup of white vinegar in a microwave-safe bowl or mug on high for about 3 minutes. Continue to let the vinegar sit inside for another 15 minutes, then remove the vinegar and wipe down the inside of the microwave with a cloth or sponge, using water.

Tip #91

(Green) Toilet Bowl Cleaner:

Swirl ½ cup white vinegar around the toilet bowl. Let stand a few minutes, scrub, and flush. Wipe toilet with homemade all-purpose cleaner and a damp microfiber cloth. For extra hard stains, add ½ cup Borax to toilet bowl water and let it soak overnight.

Tip #90

Use olive oil to dissolve tar.

Use a pencil eraser to remove heel marks.

Tip #88

Use a wet pumice stone to scrub away rust and other stains on porcelain.

Tip #87

Deodorizing your kitchen: pour a cupful of white vinegar down the kitchen drain every week and wait at least a half hour before running water to rinse. Ice cubes made from vinegar are great to place in your garbage disposal to freshen things up.

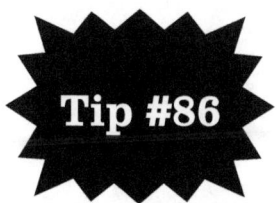

Tip #86

Deodorizing plastic Tupperware: if by chance you had food in your Tupperware bowl that left an odor, sprinkle the container with baking soda, close the container and let it sit overnight. In the morning wash, and rinse as usual. The smell will have dissipated.

Cleaning badly burned pots: Pour ¼ cup of white vinegar in the pot. Place the pot on the stove and turn the temperature to high. Pour in 2-3 Tbsp of baking soda and turn heat to low. Cook for 10 minutes. Turn off stove. Let sit for another 15 minutes, use a scrub brush to remove residue and rinse pot clean. The bottom of the pot will shine and look like new.

Household Saving
Tips 85 – 76

Tip #85

If you have a dishwasher, consider washing your dishes by hand unless you have a full load.

Tip #84

Home repairs: if they are needed, schedule during the "slow season" if possible.

Examples:

➤ Tree services and landscaping in the winter time

➤ Exterior jobs in the fall and winter; interior in the spring and summer

➤ Lawnmower tune-up in the winter

➤ Chimney swept in the summer

➤ Carpets cleaned after the holidays

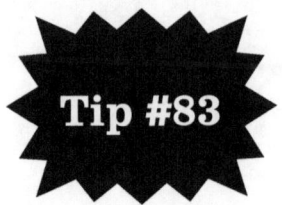

Change as many of your home light bulbs to the energy efficient ones as you can. You would be surprised how much that shaves off your utility bill.

Tip #82

Facial tissue: no need to grab two tissues when one will do. If half the tissue is un-used save it and tuck it in a safe place and use at a different time.

Tip #81

Paper towels: there is such a large waste with paper towels.

➢ You don't need several at a time when one will do

➢ If you are just drying your clean hands with a paper towel, hang it on a rack or towel bar to dry when finished and reuse at another time. Or use the towel to wipe up spills or scratches on the floor, or a spill on the counter top. You will notice a savings on your grocery bill when you buy less paper goods.

Tip #80

Speaking of paper goods, if you use plastic forks, knives or the styrofoam plates, all can be easily washed and reused if not badly soiled.

Tip #79

Toilet Paper: is a household biggie! I know of a company that created a bidet in a bottle and sells the cloths along with the product for female refreshing cleanse when going to use the bathroom (contact me if you desire additional information for the company). Not only does this method leave you refreshed, using the 100% cotton cloths saves on using toilet paper. The cloths can be rinsed out after each use and reused; then during laundry day; throw them in with the whites and wash.

Tip #78

Home insulation is one of the main savings for a home in the winter and the summer. Check your attic, basement, and crawl-
spaces to see if you have full coverage. Add-
ing insulation can cost anywhere from 15
cents to $4 per square foot, depending on
what type you use. You will not be throwing away dollars on lost heat or air in the
summer or winter time. You will find this to
be a great savings. Also check with your city
utilities. Many times they have programs to
insulate your home. Or contract with ven-
dors who will charge you less than the going
rate for the process.

An energy audit is very helpful and most city utility companies offer one for free. The waiting list maybe long but well worth the wait.

Tip #76

Use reusable rags and save the paper goods. Save old socks, t-shirts (cut in quarters) or your favorite cotton pj's that are falling apart, cut them up and use them as rags. Or you can purchase the small white hand cloths in a pack of 12 for a few dollars. They can be used again and again, and you can bleach them all when you wash.

Food Saving Tips 75 – 58

Tip #75

I am big on vitamins. When it comes to ordering, I look for the best price for the best quality. Here are several online sources:

➢ Vitacost (www.vitacost.com): sells food products, vitamins, shampoos, bath products and more. Their shipping fee is $4.99 (at the printing of this book) no matter how small or large your order is. They frequently have sales and sometimes waive the shipping fee for their brand name products.

➢ Pureformula (www.pureformula.com): does not charge shipping fees on anything and I have found the vitamins and supplements the least inexpensive as a whole.

➢ Healthdesigns (www.healthdesigns.com): is another inexpensive place to check for your vitamins.

➢ Native Remedies (www.nativeremedies. com): sells homeopathic products and

➢ Healthbeyondhype

(www.healthbeyondhype.com): has excellent quality vitamins and products that are worth a look. Shop and compare on any of these sites to find which one offers the best price for the product you are purchasing.

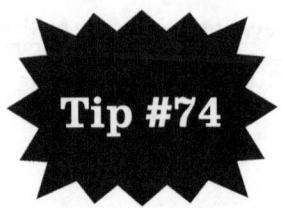

Tip #74

If you buy food items in glass jars, like, mustard, pickles, mayo, etc., you can rinse them out and use them for snacks, seasonings or other items for storage and keeping food fresh. I use them for flour, rice, nuts, carob candies, seasonings, popcorn and the list goes on. Glass is better than plastic when it comes to storage and freshness.

Tip #73

When buying products, think about buying generic products as much as possible. Many times the generic product is made by the same brand name company just without the advertised logo (which drives the price of the product). Be mindful and compare ingredients, check dosage or amount, and verify product volume and weight. Many times you will find the generic brand is cheaper and the quality remains.

Tip #72

Eat more rice or quinoa. They are cheaper and healthier than white potatoes, pasta or bread. If your grocery store has a bulk section, get these items from there as you will find the cost to be much less expensive than buying in a box or bag, and you can buy as much or as little as you desire. A dinner meal consisting of rice or quinoa topped with fresh steamed veggies, pinto, kidney or black beans or organic lentil soup (poured over the rice) is a filling meal full of protein.

Tip #71

Rinse off aluminum foil that you use when cooking in the oven if it is lightly soiled. However, once it is too soiled to reuse, ball it up and place inside of a netted bag that you purchased your oranges in and use as a scrub brush for pots and pans.

Tip #70

Rinse out lightly soiled baggies thoroughly and let dry to reuse.

Tip #69

Invest in a crockpot that you find on sale. Meals are easy and inexpensive when you cook in the pot.

Tip #68

If eating out as a family with two or more members, try ordering one main dish, an appetizer and side salad to help make a meal for two. Ordering appetizers gives additional perks to trying other items on the menu.

Tip #67

Check for "Groupon" sites or meal deals on line for restaurants in your area. Don't buy just because, only buy if you frequent the restaurant and remember to use the Groupon before the expiration date.

Tip #66

When eating out for lunch, go for the lunch specials. If you are single, purchase the lunch special, eat half for lunch and save the other half for dinner or lunch the next day. You can always make a side dish if necessary on the second day.

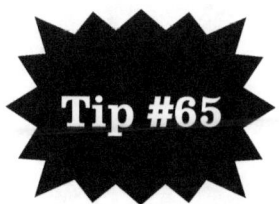

Tip #65

Bottled water is really overrated! Bottled water is subjected to less rigorous testing and purity standards than your tap water. I recommend you buy a water filter for your refrigerator and/or your kitchen sink. You will save a ton of money.

Tip #64

When buying your bread, instead of purchasing it at the grocery store, check out
your nearest bread store. It is usually half
the price that you pay at the grocery store
and still fresh. That's almost two loaves for
the price of one. You can buy several loaves
and freeze until you are ready to use them.

Tip #63

Don't be fooled or frightened by the "Sell by" date or "Best used by" date stamp on your products (see www.fsis.usda.gov).

Per the USDA on safe-to-buy and perishable grocery items:

➢ "Sell by" date tells the store how long to display the product for sale. You should buy the product before the date expires.

➢ "Best if used by (or Before)" date is recommended for best flavor or quality. It is not a purchase or safety date.

➢ "Use by" date is the last date recommended for the use of the product while at peak quality. This date is determined by the manufacturer of the product.

Tip #62

Buying your fruits and vegetables in season is much better and healthier for your family. You can freeze all of them. However, try blanching the vegetables first (place veggies in boiling water for 2 minutes, then run cold water over to stop the cooking), then place in airtight containers to store in your freezer. Remember to label and date items.

Tip #61

Think about purchasing a dehydrator. Dehydrating removes the water contained in foods and it concentrates the flavors and preserves the nutrients in a wide range of products, such as fruits, vegetables, meats, fish, nuts, etc. Once dehydrated, foods can last up to two years or longer in an airtight storage container.

Tip #60

Buy your own popcorn and pop in a paper bag. Measure out about ¼ cup popping corn, pour in a brown paper bag, and fold over the ends. Turn the microwave on and when popping stops, turn the microwave off and remove the bag from the micro-wave. You can add your favorite seasonings for a yummy healthy taste. Or, try cooking the old-fashioned way on top of the stove: heat the oil in a deep pot on top of the stove. When the oil appears to be hot (not smoking as that's too hot), pour in about a ¼ cup of popcorn. Tilt the lid just enough for the steam to ease out (this is done so the popcorn does not become chewy) and the popcorn begins to pop. Feel free to shake the pot a bit just so all the corn will pop. When the popping sound slows down, be ready to transfer the perfect popcorn into your popcorn bowl. Heat a little butter and drizzle on top, sprinkled with a little of your favorite seasoning and Voilá! a delish snack.

Tip #59

Your fruits (such as berries, strawberries, blackberries, etc.) will last longer if you place them in your sink filled with water and about a ½ cup of plain old distilled white vinegar (whatever is cheap or store brand) in the water. Put in the fruits to be rinsed. Leave them in the sink about 5 minutes then drain the water. The fruits will not have a vinegar taste, but you can rinse if you desire. Washing them in vinegar water will extend the freshness and the fruit will last 1-2 weeks longer.

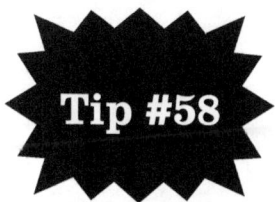

Tip #58

If you love salads like I do, then you buy a lot of greens; spinach, red lettuce, kale, really any of your greens; you can prepare by washing in salt water, rinse, dry by paper towel or salad spinner. To regulate the moisture in the plastic tub that you use to store the greens, tear a paper towel in half and line the bottom of the container, then add the greens and cover them with the other half of the paper towel before putting the lid on. If possible don't store your greens in the produce bags from the grocery store as the greens tend to rapidly wilt and get slimy.

Clothing Tips 57 – 54

Tip #57

Dress for the temp at hand! If you are at home in the summer, put on a pair of shorts and a t-shirt instead of turning on the air-conditioner to cool things off. Or at least keep the thermostat on 80 degrees. When you are in a room, turning on the ceiling fan to move the air around will help to keep your skin cool. In the winter months, do just the opposite. Put on a jogging suit and socks and turn the thermostat to 68 degrees. You will find these temperatures help lower your utility bill tremendously. You will be glad you did at the end of the month.

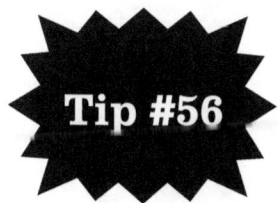

Tip #56

When you buy an article of clothing for any-one in your household, be sure to remove one piece (or however many pieces you purchased) from the closet to make room for the new ones you purchased. This will help you to recycle the items and give to your favorite charity, avoiding clutter in your house and giving you a helpful tax write off at year end if you qualify.

Save the spare buttons on garments, shirts, dresses or suits. You can use them to make earrings or necklaces to match the outfits, use them in scrapbooking, use them to create eyes for dolls, and for a host of other creative ideas.

Tip #54

Dry cleaning is big money. Look for Groupons, use coupons or, better, hand wash in cold water if possible the delicate items. If it is a suit or clothing with lining or something of that nature, try using Dryel or Swash (they make a clothing dewrinkler, clothing odor and stain remover sheets). You can treat several items at once with these products.

Automotive Saving
Tips 53 – 47

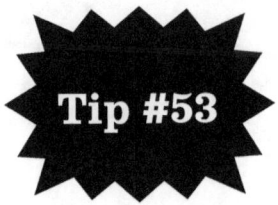

Tip #53

While driving around town, to save on gas, drive the lower end of the speed limit. Do **Not** speed up to the red lights; take your foot off the brake and coast to the light. Try not to accelerate when the light turns green as that alone burns a lot of fuel. Consider carpooling, combining trips when you leave the house, walking or biking to the stores or work when you can. I fill up every three weeks (and I have a Toyota Camry). That saves me a ton of money, considering the gas prices these days.

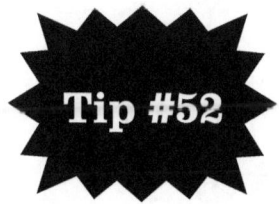

Tip #52

Buy regular gas unless you have a high performance car.

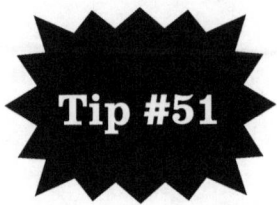

Tip #51

Buy a used car if possible – saves you the hassle of working out the bugs.

Tip #50

Create a "Thank You" Car Fund: keep an envelope in an inconspicuous place in your car, and pay it a dollar every day or more if you can. And when you are placing the money in the envelope, thank your car for running so well and getting you around in a safe manner. Just showing appreciation. You can use the money in a pinch or continue to save it up when you need gas for the car, or when repairs are necessary.

Tip #49

Keep your oil changed as prescribed by your car manufacturer to extend the life of the car.

Tip #48

Have your tires rotated every other oil change and make sure the tire pressure is checked. This will save gas, which keeps more money in your pocket for other expenses. Your car is only as good as you treat it.

Tip #47

Take advantage of Zipcars: they are in most major cities and a lot of college towns. Zipcar is a car share program. You pay a nominal annual fee for 24/7 access to a fleet of vehicles parked in lots scattered across the city. You make a reservation by phone or online and use an electronic keycard to access the car. You pay by the hour or day. Gas, insurance, maintenance, parking registration and taxes are the company's responsibility.

Insurance Tips (car, house, life, medical) 46 – 44

Tip #46

Sometimes bundling your auto and home-owner's insurance into a package policy saves you money, but check on both separately to make sure. Also raising your deductibles for car insurance, health insurance or homeowner's insurance you will find helps to lower your premium payment, which saves you money.

Tip #45

When purchasing your Rx drugs, check with the warehouse stores like Costco, Sam's Club or BJ's Wholesale Club. You don't have to be a member to purchase your prescriptions there. Many times their cost is a true bargain. You may have to see management since they check ID at the door, but you should have no problem once you have done so.

Tip #44

Health Insurance – if you are in good health, consider purchasing your insurance with a large annual deductible. This will lower your monthly payments. What you save on the purchase of the insurance you might consider placing in a savings fund for the health expenses you may incur.

Plain Old Saving
Tips 43 – 34

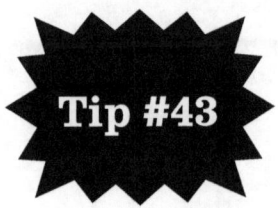

Tip #43

Do you have a shredder at home? If so, instead of throwing away the shredded paper, you can use it for packing materials to ship.

Bonus

Do you associate bartering with a bygone era? Bartering is simply trading goods and services without the use of money. Think about some skills or services that you have to offer others. Here's a few real life examples – a web designer trades services with a dentist for cosmetic dental procedures, families exchange child and elder care services on a regular basis, a hairstylist trades services with a professional chef for home cooked meals once a week, and a manicurist provides services for her gardener's wife once a week.

Tip #42

Think twice about marrying someone who does not know or is not interested in saving money.

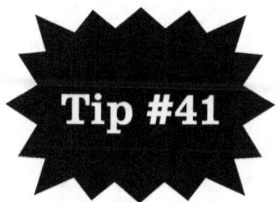

Tip #41

If you have a home copy machine, you can use the copy blunders for note taking paper.

Do you buy a lot of books? It may be well worth your efforts to invest in an Amazon. com membership of $79 a year. I do not work for Amazon, but I have found that their membership pays for itself throughout the year. Not only do I order books, I also order vitamins, computer parts and cell phones. You name it, Amazon sells it, and because I am an Amazon prime member, I also have access to online free movies. There must be over 4,000 movies I can access for free. Amazon is the cheapest place overall where I have found to buy books. If your purchase is under $25, you do not have to pay for shipping. If you buy an Amazon Prime book, shipping is free. Also on Amazon, you can sell products like you can on eBay, and there is no charge to sell them on Amazon.

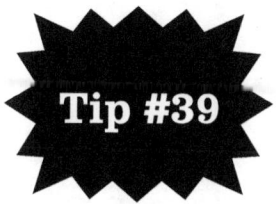

Check the following websites to purchase used items of all kinds: www.freecycle.org and www.craigslist.org. Check out your local Goodwill and Habitat for Humanity stores for drastically discounted items. If at all possible, buy used or at least buy out of season when the items are sold at a lower price.

Tip #38

There's money hiding in your home, from all the items that you haven't used or worn in the last 6 months to a year. Have a garage sale. Now is the time to de-clutter your home. The money you make can be put towards any number of things: buying gas, groceries or paying off some of your bills.

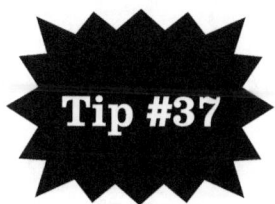

Tip #37

If your employer has a 401(k) matching con-
tribution program, you should by all means
take advantage of it. If you don't, it's like
throwing money away.

Tip #36

Shop for Christmas all during the year. Make up your Christmas list, then throughout the year as you are in the stores, keep your list handy in your purse or wallet in case there are items on your list on sale. That would be the perfect time to buy. Then mark off your list. Spreading out your shopping efforts throughout the year will help to relieve the burden and misappropriation of funds at the end of the year.

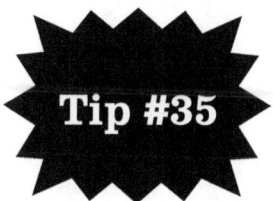

Tip #35

Paying off your home early sounds like a financially smart move; however, when you pay your mortgage, you are using after-tax dollars, which means that for every $1 you make, only 70 cents or so goes to the bank. Consider this: contributing pre-tax dollars to your 401(k), so the full buck goes in. Your money is compounding, you are keeping more of the money you earned and when entering retirement you can pay off your house with the 401(k) and still have peace of mind in your retirement years.

By using this Saving Chart you could save $855 in one year; either from your pay check, or Tip #100, Tip #50 or Tip #38.

52 Week Money Saving Challenge

Week	Deposit Amount	Account Balance	Week	Deposit Amount	Account Balance
1	$5	$5	28	$50	$275
4	$10	$15	31	$55	$330
7	$15	$30	34	$60	$390
10	$20	$50	37	$65	$455
13	$25	$75	40	$70	$525
16	$30	$105	43	$75	$600
19	$35	$140	46	$80	$680
22	$40	$180	49	$85	$765
25	$45	$225	52	$90	$855

Garden Saving Tips 34 – 29

Tip #34

A mixture of vinegar and dish soap kills weeds – make your own weed-killing solution by mixing vinegar with a bit of food-safe dish soap. Just fill an old spray bottle and apply directly onto your weeds.

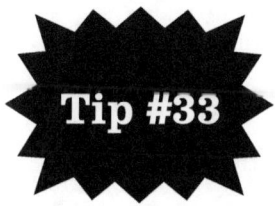

Tip #33

Water your lawn only when it needs it. Step on your grass. If it springs back when you lift your foot, it doesn't need water. Consider converting your lawn to native plants. This is also a cost-effective measure.

Tip #32

Set your lawn mower blades at the highest notch. Longer grass means less evaporation of water and could save you from 500 – 1,000 gallons each month.

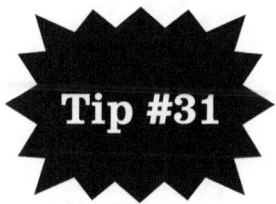

Tip #31

If you have an evaporative air conditioner, direct the water drain line to a flower bed, tree base or lawn.

Tip #30

If you decide to wash your car at home, drive it on the lawn. That way excess water will water the grass.

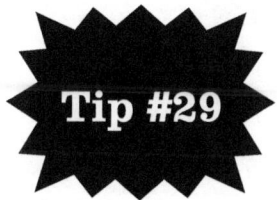

Tip #29

If you allow your children to play in the sprinklers, make sure it is on a day you have designated to water the lawn.

Water Saving Tips 28 – 22

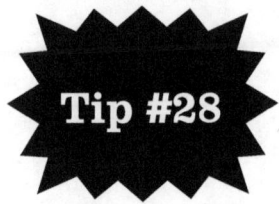

Tip #28

Fix leaky faucets and plumbing joints. This could save you as much as 20 gallons per day for every leak stopped.

Tip #27

While washing your car, don't keep the hose running. Use a bucket of water and a quick hose rinse at the end. That saves about 150 gallons each time.

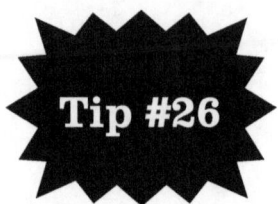

Install water-saving shower heads. Shortening your shower use by 1-2 minutes could save you up to 700 gallons of water per month.

Tip #25

Use your washing machine and dishwasher with full loads. This could save you up to 300 to 800 gallons per month.

Here's a doozy! Put a plastic bottle or a plastic bag weighted with pebbles and filled with water in your toilet tank. Displacing the water will use less water with each flush which could save you from 5-10 gallons a day.

Tip #23

Turn off the water while brushing your teeth, shaving or washing your face. Just letting it run while you are doing these activities wastes water. Turning it off can save you about 3 gallons.

Tip #22

If you only wash clothes every two weeks, try unplugging your washer and dryer. In fact, unplug all electrical appliances that are not in use on a daily basis. That could be a savings of up to 10% on your utility bill.

Skin Care Tips 21 – 20

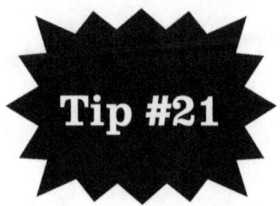

Use cold-pressed olive oil as an inexpensive make up remover and as natural wrinkle prevention if you have dry skin.

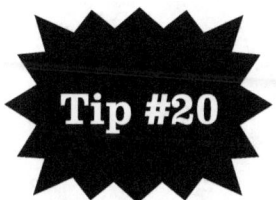

Tip #20

Stretch your lotion. If you use or have cheap lotion that is runny but has a nice fragrance, mix it with the store brand baby oil (or a natural oil like sweet oil) to thicken it up and it will last longer.

Entertainment Saving
Tips 19 – 14

Do you like the theater, opera, or musicals? Think of volunteering at your church, the local non-profit theater, the local community center and the fringe benefit will be to see the show.

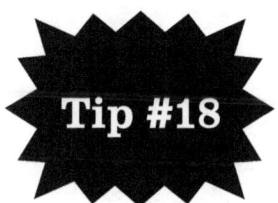

Tip #18

If you enjoy home remodeling, gardening, cooking, or sewing, why not turn these "projects" into entertainment activities? Invite some friends over to enjoy the projects with you, have a potluck with others who enjoy your hobby and presto! You've created an inexpensive and entertaining social activity that others look forward to.

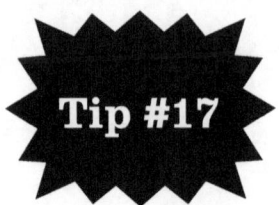

Love to make scrapbooks? If you are like me you hate throwing away your Christmas cards or Birthday cards, save them for scrap-booking. You can use the front side with the beautiful picture and decorate a page in your scrapbook. You may have a winter scene that you would like to display in your scrapbook "Family Home for the Holidays". You get the idea.

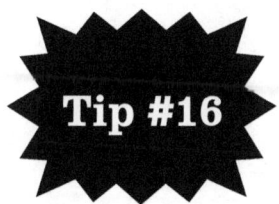

Tip #16

Michael's, Hobby Lobby, Home Depot, etc. offer craft or garden classes on a weekly basis for free or a small fee.

Tip #15

Public libraries, museums, parks, universities or community colleges offer free lectures, computer access and facilities. Several library websites provide free music, ebook and movie downloads. Library story times, DVDs and video games provide hours of free entertainment for the little ones!

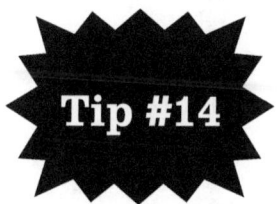

Tip #14

If you love movies like I do, Netflix is a bar-gain! For a fee as little as $8.99 a month, you choose from over 100,000 movie titles, seminars, instructional videos, one at a time and sent through the mail. You can watch as often as you like and invite over as many friends as you like. Also, don't forget your public library has all the latest movies for free (although you may have to wait a little longer to check them out). Maybe a movie night is in order for the family.

Travel Saving Tips 13 – 2

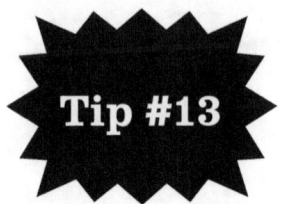

Tip #13

When traveling by air, use you're airline points whenever possible. Don't forget, you're earning them to pay for future trips!

Tip #12

Do the same for your hotel stays. The points can go a long way and get you extra free nights in hotel rooms. If you have the discipline to pay off your credit cards at the end of each month, then make sure to use the credit cards that offer the greatest rewards to you and your family when you travel (points for air or hotel stays). Here's another credit card suggestion - consider using the credit cards to pay your bills every month but only if you have the discipline to pay off the credit card bill each month! Groceries, gas, and other purchases can be paid by credit card to earn points, but again, only consider this tip if you can pay off the entire balance each month!

Tip #11

Traveling off-season is always the greatest bargain. Before you travel, contact the Chamber of Commerce to obtain a free packet of information for the area. The packet usually comes with discount coupons or special offers for the local hotels, restaurants and other attractions. Also purchase an Entertainment Book (www.entertainment.com) for the area. This book is usually packed with specials, coupons, etc., for lodging, restaurants and attractions.

Souvenir shopping: you may find it interesting to shop at a local Goodwill, thrift store or consignment shop. Also, large chain stores like Walmart offer local souvenirs at deep discounts.

Tip #9

Airline fares: Simply driving to another air-
port in your area can help you find a better
airfare. Also, booking your flight for a late
Tuesday, Wednesday or Saturday departure
can also yield savings.

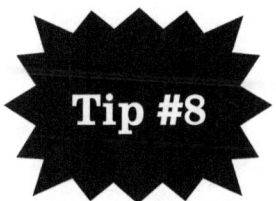

Tip #8

Since the airlines do not allow liquid beverages past the check point, carry your empty water bottle with you (consider a filtered water bottle option if that is a concern). Once you clear the check point, you can fill it at the water fountain, or at a large fountain drink that gives refills. Fill your water bottle with the beverage.

Tip #7

Car Rentals: I have found a great website www.carrentals.com with the best car rental prices overall. More recently, I use websites that don't require a credit card to make a reservation. This is helpful if I change my mind about the rental, or find something better. Check with your auto insurance carrier and credit card company in advance to avoid duplicating any coverage you may already have.

Bonus

Transportation: When you are on vacation or a business trip and need transportation, a rental car or taxi is always available; however, don't forget about public transportation. The cost is very economical and will get you from point A to point B. The local transportation authorities are usually very helpful when you provide an address or area you would like to travel.

Tip #6

Have you ever considered renting a condo or a home directly from the homeowner as an alternative to a traditional hotel room? Then check out www.VRBO.com (Vacation Rentals by Owner). This website allows you to rent directly from the owner, whether you're talking about a home, condo, cabin, villa or apartment. Use the reviews from previous customers on the rentals as a guide.

Bonus

Want a free place to stay while on vacation? Become a house-sitter! There are several websites where you can apply to become a house-sitter. If you can locate a home in the area of your desire you will have free housing while vacationing.

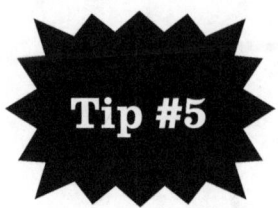

Tip #5

When traveling and packing your jewelry, forget those expensive jewelry organizers and use a straw to pack your necklaces so that they won't tangle. You can cut the straw in half for bracelets.

Tip #4

Also use the twist ties from your fruit or bulk item purchases at the grocery store to keep all of your rings/jewelry together so that you can find them easily.

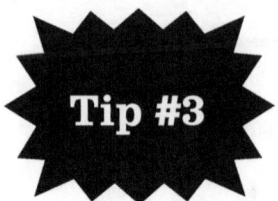

Tip #3

Instead of taking your vitamin jars or pill bottles in your luggage (which causes bulk and could add to the weight of the bag), use zip lock baggies and label them with the name and dosage if necessary.

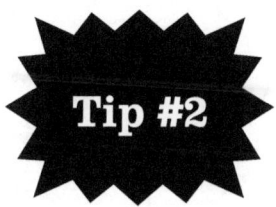

Tip #2

Enroll in the survey sites like www.ere-wards.com and www.emiles.com. You can build up your points and turn them into skymiles with your airline carrier, or hotel points with your favorite hotel, or gift cards at stores like Macy's, Starbuck's, Amazon.com and more.

Relationships Tip 1

Tip #1

Last but surely not least...

Love can cause money problems—but not the ones you might expect. Most individuals utilize an internal financial math that makes their budget work: some people like me cut corners on the things they don't care about and splurge on things they value. For instance, I'm perfectly happy keeping my grocery bill low. If I have to eat beans and rice five days out of the week, I do. Yet I love going to the movies any time day or night. So I do splurge on paying the extra exuberant price for the movies. Then if I fall for a guy who is a gourmet cook and would rather watch movies on TV, he might spend $100 at the grocery store for a week. It's easy to start sharing each other's pleasures, but hard to give up our own. The result - as a couple, you pile on the new expenses while abandoning your former budgeting strategies. Asking your partner to stop doing the things that make him or her happy is a great way to build resentment and encourage financial infidelity. So instead, start with the fun stuff: Come up with a list of what you both value most and together build a budget that will help you achieve those goals. During that process, you'll each have to make sacrifices, but it won't feel as if your partner is living it up while you are being denied.

Did you know that for 50 years, up until 1966, America celebrated National Thrift Week? It was a celebration of all things non-commercial. The slogan at the time was "For Success and Happiness". There was a celebration every year on January 17 (birthday of Benjamin Franklin, the advocate of thrift).

There was a different theme for every day of the week: Have a Bank Account Day, Invest Safely Day, Carry Life Insurance Day, Keep a Budget Day, Pay Bills Promptly Day, Own Your Home Day, and Share with Others Day. Maybe it's time to re-activate some of these old habits in your own life. They are yet another easy tool to help you get back to basics and get on the road to "Financial Well Being".

So, what have I learned personally from developing "100 Timeless Money Saving Tips"??? I learned that:

- It's definitely okay to spend money, while remembering to think of money as a tool. Use it well and wisely, and it will work for you.

- Saving in one area allows you the option to enjoy in other areas.

- Being consciously aware of your spending habits is the first step to more freedom. Often this awareness gives you a quantum

www.bethechange.org

www.everywomansmoney.com (a blog for women's expression about money)

www.braveheartwoman.com (15-minute conversations to inspire women on all sorts of topics)

www.retailmenot.com (coupons from many retailers)

www.groupon.com

www.livingsocial.com

ABOUT THE AUTHOR

LaTanya Hicks is author of the book, "100 Timeless Money Saving Tips" and a professional Budget Solutions Consultant. Her passion is to assist her clients in developing long-term, financial strategies to get them out of debt and maintain financial freedom! While LaTanya's clients have diverse backgrounds and financial challenges, many share some common challenges that she is able to effectively address.

If any of the following life situations sound familiar, you may benefit from LaTanya's proven services:

- Next month's bills arrive and last month's bills remain unpaid

- Bill payments and late fees go hand-in-hand each month

- You avoid opening monthly bills and feel overwhelmed by rising debt

- You prefer to have a root canal without anesthesia to balancing your checkbook on a regular basis

- Bounced checks are a frequent and embarrassing occurrence

- You frequently use payday, car title and other high interest loans to cover your expenses

- At the end of each month, you're not sure where your money went

Being afraid or ashamed...is not a solution.

Thinking you can do it all alone... is not a solution.

Doing nothing at all...is not a solution.

LaTanya's philosophy and proven solutions are based on the belief that - **You can't solve a problem with the same mindset that created it!** She believes the key to getting out of these situations is to act now. Taking charge of your finances and creating a plan for tackling the debt will cut out anxiety and place you on a path to a healthier financial future.

If interested you may contact her office at 918-533-9288 or by email at <u>latanya.hicks@com cast.net</u>

NOTES

NOTES